# AMERICAN HORROR STORY

## THE ULTIMATE QUIZ BOOK

### JACK GOLDSTEIN & FRANKIE TAYLOR

Published in 2016 by
**Acorn Books**
www.acornbooks.co.uk
Acorn Books is an imprint of
**Andrews UK Limited**
www.andrewsuk.com

# CONTENTS

| Questions | | Answers |
|---|---|---|

| About the Show | 3 | 71 |
| Pot Luck – Part 1 | 4 | 72 |
| Just Who – Part 1 | 5 | 73 |
| Random Selection – Part 1 | 6 | 74 |
| Episode Names – Part 1 | 7 | 75 |
| People – Part 1 | 8 | 76 |
| Actors and Actresses – Part 1 | 9 | 77 |
| Objects – Part 1 | 10 | 78 |
| Characters – Part 1 | 11 | 79 |
| Who Am I? – Part 1 | 12 | 80 |
| Locations – Part 1 | 14 | 81 |
| Quotes – Part 1 | 15 | 82 |
| Whose Death – Part 1 | 16 | 83 |
| Random Selection – Part 2 | 17 | 84 |
| Death & Killing – Part 1 | 18 | 85 |
| Pot Luck – Part 2 | 19 | 86 |
| Episode Names – Part 2 | 20 | 87 |
| Just Who – Part 2 | 21 | 88 |
| Names – Part 1 | 22 | 89 |
| People – Part 2 | 23 | 90 |
| Objects – Part 2 | 24 | 91 |
| Jobs & Occupations | 25 | 92 |
| Numbers – Part 1 | 26 | 93 |
| Locations – Part 2 | 27 | 94 |
| Random Selection – Part 3 | 28 | 95 |
| Actors and Actresses – Part 2 | 29 | 96 |
| Quotes – Part 2 | 30 | 97 |
| Pot Luck – Part 3 | 31 | 98 |
| Characters – Part 2 | 32 | 99 |
| Who Am I? – Part 2 | 33 | 100 |
| Food & Drink | 34 | 101 |
| Episode Names – Part 3 | 35 | 102 |
| Just Who – Part 3 | 36 | 103 |

# CONTENTS (CONT.)

**Questions**  **Answers**

People – Part 3 . . . . . . . . . . . . . . . . . 37 . . . . . . . . . . . .104

Random Selection – Part 4 . . . . . . . 38 . . . . . . . . . . . .105

Objects – Part 3 . . . . . . . . . . . . . . . 39 . . . . . . . . . . . .106

Locations – Part 3 . . . . . . . . . . . . . 40 . . . . . . . . . . . .107

Pot Luck – Part 4 . . . . . . . . . . . . . . 41 . . . . . . . . . . . .108

True or False. . . . . . . . . . . . . . . . . . 42 . . . . . . . . . . . .109

Actors and Actresses – Part 3 . . . . . 43 . . . . . . . . . . . .110

Characters – Part 3 . . . . . . . . . . . . 44 . . . . . . . . . . . .111

Random Selection – Part 5 . . . . . . . 45 . . . . . . . . . . . .112

Episode Names – Part 4. . . . . . . . . 46 . . . . . . . . . . . .113

Objects – Part 4 . . . . . . . . . . . . . . . 47 . . . . . . . . . . . .114

Just Who – Part 4. . . . . . . . . . . . . . 48 . . . . . . . . . . . .115

Pot Luck – Part 5 . . . . . . . . . . . . . . 49 . . . . . . . . . . . .116

Names – Part 2. . . . . . . . . . . . . . . . 50 . . . . . . . . . . . .117

Quotes – Part 3. . . . . . . . . . . . . . . . 51 . . . . . . . . . . . .118

Who Am I? – Part 3. . . . . . . . . . . . . 52 . . . . . . . . . . . .119

Whose Death Is This? – Part 2 . . . . 54 . . . . . . . . . . . .120

Random Selection – Part 6 . . . . . . . 55 . . . . . . . . . . . .121

Costumes . . . . . . . . . . . . . . . . . . . . 56 . . . . . . . . . . . .122

Locations – Part 4 . . . . . . . . . . . . . 57 . . . . . . . . . . . .123

Numbers – Part 2. . . . . . . . . . . . . . 58 . . . . . . . . . . . .124

Death & Killing – Part 2 . . . . . . . . . 59 . . . . . . . . . . . .125

Objects – Part 5 . . . . . . . . . . . . . . . 60 . . . . . . . . . . . .126

Characters – Part 4 . . . . . . . . . . . . . 61 . . . . . . . . . . . .127

Actors and Actresses – Part 4 . . . . . 62 . . . . . . . . . . . .128

People – Part 4 . . . . . . . . . . . . . . . . 63 . . . . . . . . . . . .129

Episode Names – Part 5. . . . . . . . . 64 . . . . . . . . . . . .130

Pot Luck – Part 6 . . . . . . . . . . . . . . 65 . . . . . . . . . . . .131

Just Who – Part 5. . . . . . . . . . . . . . 66 . . . . . . . . . . . .132

Random Selection – Part 7 . . . . . . . 67 . . . . . . . . . . . .133

# INTRODUCTION

With so much to cover over six seasons, we decided the best way to organise the quiz was to have rounds that focus on certain categories rather than split the sections up by season – we feel it is much more fun this way. Of course, that means a section can contain questions about any of the six seasons. To make sure you don't get confused (particularly as some characters have similar names) at the end of each question you'll see a number in brackets; this corresponds with the season to which the question refers.

We hope that you have as much fun reading this quiz as we had writing it. We are grateful to the creators of the show (who we won't name here considering it is one of the first questions) for giving us many hours of fantastic viewing. Having covered the first six seasons in this book, we'd love it if we could do the same for the *next* six seasons… well, one can hope!

We won't keep you waiting any longer though, so thank you for buying this book… and on with the quiz. Good luck!

# THE QUIZ

# THE QUESTIONS

# ABOUT THE SHOW

*First up, a few questions about the show in general...*

1. Name each season in ascending order, using the fan's title for season one.

2. Who are the two main creators of the show?

3. On what date did the show debut in the US?

4. Which episode out of the entirety of seasons one to six had the highest viewing figures?

5. Out of 230 award nominations received, how many had *American Horror Story* won: 11, 59, 102 or 229?

6. Which cast member won an Emmy for *Outstanding Lead Actress in a Miniseries*?

7. Which of the first six seasons was the most watched overall?

8. Who first announced what the name of the fifth season was going to be?

9. What were the televised teasers for Season two called that featured cast members lying in beds and talking to the cameras?

10. What is the name of the exhibit that is to be created at Universal Studios featuring a walk-through maze of various sets and themes from the show?

*See page 71 for the answers*

# POT LUCK – PART 1

*These questions can be about any subject from any season, so get your thinking caps on, these will __really__ test your memory...*

11. How did Twisty's face become disfigured? [4]

12. What three past transgressions does the demon taunt Sister Jude with during the exorcism? [2]

13. What is the name of the company that Marcy works for? [1]

14. Which wonder couldn't Queenie perform for her test? [3]

15. When Twisty performs for his captives, what causes him to fly into a wild rage? [4]

16. How does Sister Jude initially attempt to punish Shelley for her transgressions? [2]

17. When Nan summons the council, why does she believe Madison is dead? [3]

18. Which of Dot's talents is Elsa rather surprised at? [4]

19. What caused Twisty's mental disability? [4]

20. How did Elsa torture the soldier in the story she tells to Mordrake? [4]

*See page 72 for the answers*

# JUST WHO – PART 1

*All of these questions quite simply ask who did something, said something or had something done to them...*

21. Who deals the final killing blow to one of the Bloody Faces: Leo or Teresa? [2]

22. Who recites the incantation that returns Spalding's tongue to his mouth? [3]

23. Who is the first person that Todd and his friends come across in the woods? [6]

24. Who does Lee manipulate in order to escape? [6]

25. Who was the first member of *Fräulein Elsa's Cabinet of Curiosities*? [4]

26. Who smothered Beauregard with a pillow? [1]

27. Who is Spivey watching bathe when Dr Arden catches him in a rather compromising situation? [2]

28. Who is the only Roanoke victim to die by suicide? [6]

29. Who does Hayden have a brief affair with... before killing him? [1]

30. Who is killed to complete the Janes' word game? [6]

*See page 73 for the answers*

# RANDOM SELECTION – PART 1

*Another pot-luck style round here; cast your mind back and try to remember the answers to these increasingly difficult questions...*

31.  Cordelia enchants Queenie's ticket for which show? [3]

32.  Why does Will cover Lachlan's eyes during their tour of the hotel? [5]

33.  What caused Madison to kill a movie director? [3]

34.  On what do Max's friends Maddy and Jimmy blame the carnage at school? [5]

35.  What does Leah tell Violet she thinks she saw in the basement? [1]

36.  What song does Nan tell Joan that Luke wants her to sing? [3]

37.  Which word is left sprayed on the wall by Miranda and Bridget? [6]

38.  In what year was Elizabeth born? [5]

39.  In which magazine is a spread about a Halloween performance promised? [4]

40.  How did Elsa lose her legs? [4]

*See page 74 for the answers*

# EPISODE NAMES – PART 1

*These are all the names of episodes from American Horror Story... but from which season?*

41. *Boy Parts*

42. *Flicker*

43. *Burn, Witch. Burn!*

44. *Smouldering Children*

45. *Checking In*

46. *Rubber Man*

47. *Nor'easter*

48. *Birth*

49. *Bitchcraft*

50. *Tupperware Party Massacre*

*See page 75 for the answers*

# IT'S ALL ABOUT THE PEOPLE – PART 1

*These questions are all about the characters in the show; questions cover all six seasons so far...*

51. Name the hit-and-run victim who haunts Sister Jude's thoughts. [2]

52. Whose story makes Mordrake's second face weep? [4]

53. With which famous female singer does Fiona have a close relationship? [3]

54. In the 1960s, who is first believed to be Bloody Face? [2]

55. Whose flesh is Mama Polk's jerky made out of? [6]

56. Who do we find out has taken Chester's dummy? [4]

57. Who tries to kill Bartholomew in order to get revenge on his mother? [3]

58. Whose ghost does Billie Dean Howard speak to on Devil's Night for her TV Show? [5]

59. Whose disappearance does Jack Colquitt investigate in *Murder House*? [1]

60. Name the Harmon family's dog. [1]

*See page 76 for the answers*

# ACTORS AND ACTRESSES – PART 1

*How much attention do you pay to the credits... or the celebrity magazines? Let's find out! Who plays the following characters...*

61. Maggie Esmerelda [4]

62. Vivien Harmon [1]

63. Dr. Arthur Arden [2]

64. Ramona Royale [5]

65. Sister Mary Eunice [2]

66. Grace Bertrand [2]

67. Elsa Mars [4]

68. Jimmy Darling [4]

69. Elizabeth [5]

70. Madison Montgomery [3]

*See page 77 for the answers*

# OBJECTS – PART 1

*These questions are about various objects used throughout the show... kind of obvious by the round's title really...*

71. What rather 'unique' object is Stanley trying to sell to the museum? [4]

72. Which book of the Bible does Leah find particularly relevant to her experience? [1]

73. What is it that Sister Mary says is wrong with Sister Jude's cane? [2]

74. Who lights candles to get rid of the bad smell: Agnetha or Vendela? [5]

75. The first time we see Tate write on Violet's chalk board, what single word does he scrawl? [1]

76. Why was Patrick not a fan of the 'Rubber Man' suit? [1]

77. What does Delphine use to knock out Queenie? [3]

78. What gift does Liz give to Hazel Evers? [5]

79. Constance tells Moira she will keep stealing silverware until what happens? [1]

80. Which book brings Dandy to tears? [4]

*See page 78 for the answers*

# CHARACTERS – PART 1

*In which season did we first meet the following characters...*

81.  Nan

82.  Travis Wanderly

83.  Wendy Peyser

84.  Chester Creb

85.  Hazel Evers

86.  Adelaide Langdon

87.  Shelley

88.  Gabriel

89.  Marcy

90.  The Minotaur

*See page 79 for the answers*

# WHO AM I? – PART 1

*Below you will find ten paragraphs, each describing a different character from the show. All you have to do is figure out which one it is in each case...*

91. Ambitious yet careless, my plan goes horribly wrong when I attempt to go undercover one night in the hope of earning my prize. Becoming a patient was one thing, but what lay ahead was far worse. [2]

92. At the request of my mother, Dr Charles Montgomery tried (and failed) to abort me. Now I remain severely disfigured and in a permanent state of infancy. [5]

93. Once a promiscuous nightclub singer, I injured a young girl during one drink-driving accident... then because of another, I ended up on the doorstep of the church – and my life changed forever. [2]

94. Thaddeus was punishment for what we had done to those poor girls. The only option left was to the pull the trigger on both him and me. [1]

95. With my vision taken away, I was granted with another type of sight. [3]

96. Dressed in rags and covered in dirt and blood I have a strong sexual appetite; I love nothing more than a hapless man. [6]

97. At first some thought I was a figment of Flora's imagination, but it wasn't long before people realised I was a real girl, sacrificed long ago by the Roanoke colonists. [6]

98. There's nothing mystic about this Meg... in fact, it's just my extremely observant nature that enables me to give accurate readings. [4]

99. You could say I have a split personality; whereas others may be driven insane by the voices *inside* their heads, the voice that talks to *me* comes from the other side! [4]

100. I told her she was an empty collector of people and that we were in love... but her response was to slit my throat. For years afterwards I couldn't bring myself to visit Liz; I wanted her to live her life but now..? *Now* we can be in love for evermore. [5]

*See page 80 for the answers*

# LOCATIONS – PART 1

*These rounds focus on the various locations seen and spoken about within the show...*

101. What is the name of the house in which Dandy resides? [4]

102. What modern-day business does the Voodoo Queen run? [3]

103. Queenie is unhappy with her hotel room; which two words does she use to describe the negative feeling she gets from it? [5]

104. Where did Queenie work before being enrolled in the academy? [3]

105. What links Coven's academy and the Murder House? [1/3]

106. Which ride are Vendela and Agnetha particularly keen to visit? [5]

107. Which school is Scarlett eventually sent to? [5]

108. Why did Agnetha come to LA? [5]

109. To which location is Mother Claudia sent after speaking with the press? [2]

110. Where does Luke finally manage to take refuge from the zombies? [3]

*See page 81 for the answers*

# QUOTES – PART 1

*How good is your memory for dialogue? Let's find out. Who said the following lines...*

111. "You know how this goes. You make a sound; I bash your face in." [2]

112. "She's not harmless; she drowned her sister's baby and sliced his ears off!" [2]

113. "Don't worry, she won't bite. I took her teeth." [2]

114. "I shall not stand by and watch thou shed another drop of innocent blood." [6]

115. "If you're about to diagnose me with post traumatic shock syndrome, I'm going to bash your goddamn face in." [1]

116. "This place is bat-shit crazy, you know. Weird things go down, especially at night." [5]

117. "I want terms defined. Life everlasting, no ageing, no decrepitude, forever." [3]

118. "Your boy has a jawline for days!" [5]

119. "Your future's bright, I'm just not in it." [4]

120. "I wept for the state of this world, a world of lies, a world that makes promises it cannot keep. To tell a colored man that he can be equal to a white man, there's a real cruelty. I'm not going anywhere." [3]

*See page 82 for the answers*

# WHOSE DEATH IS THIS? – PART 1

*The show certainly has its fill of grizzly deaths. But can you remember which characters joined the choir invisible in these particular ways...*

121. Awakened in Houdini's water tank, but won't be performing any disappearing acts now. [4]

122. This character's throat is slit, but *one* death just isn't enough for an out-of-control Hollywood starlet. [3]

123. Harbouring resentment towards his mother and continuing his father's work, an unstable life is ended with a simple bullet to the head. [2]

124. Shot in the head by a jealous Elizabeth after a brief moment of girl-on-girl intimacy. [5]

125. Strangled by Monsignor Howard's rosary beads in an 'act of mercy' after he was called upon to read the last rites. [2]

126. Killed in a bus crash... but doesn't stay dead for long. [3]

127. After waking in the dungeons, this character is persuaded to free a vampire... who promptly kills him for his blood. [5]

128. During a game of tag, this character unexpectedly transmutes onto the top of an iron gate, becoming rather tragically impaled. [3]

129. Burned at the stake watched by both coven and council [3]

130. Burned alive atop of the woman he once loved. [2]

*See page 83 for the answers*

131. How long had Edward Mott been living in the house before finding his artwork destroyed: a couple of days, a couple of weeks or a couple of months? [6]

132. What is the name of the ghost-hunting show that goes to the house to see if the stories are true? [6]

133. How does Marcy want to spend her eternal existence in the hotel? [5]

134. What is the first thing that Nan uses her telekinesis power for? [3]

135. On what type of cases does Cricket claim to have worked on for the FBI? [6]

136. What two things does Madison do in the hope that she will 'feel' something? [3]

137. What did Scathach take in exchange for saving Thomasin's life from a wild boar? [6]

138. What is the news story Queenie and Nan watch the morning after they arrive at the academy? [3]

139. What act do we see Elsa practising for her upcoming TV show? [4]

140. Why was the Roanoke house originally built? [6]

*See page 84 for the answers*

# DEATH & KILLING – PART 1

*A great round for those with rather morbid interests...*

141. How was the Janes' first victim killed? [6]

142. Which method of killing does Chester's dummy suggest to him for the twins? [4]

143. How long had Corey's parents been dead for when they were found, according to the radio announcement? [4]

144. How does Desiree escape being killed by Dandy? [4]

145. Of what did Max Ellison almost die? [5]

146. How did Iris kill Sally? [5]

147. What did Moira do to help her mother die? [1]

148. Why did Constance want Beau killed? [1]

149. After shooting Hugo, what did his wife do to his body? [1]

150. Is the Infantata (Thaddeus Montgomery) alive or dead? [1]

*See page 85 for the answers*

# POT LUCK — PART 2

*Another round of tricky questions designed to test your memory of the entire show...*

151. With which tune does Elsa serenade Paul? [4]

152. How is Max Ellison cured of his near-deadly condition? [5]

153. Who described themselves as 'a Guardian of veracity in the vernacular'? [3]

154. What did Thomasin eat that allowed her to regain her strength? [6]

155. Of which chapter is Kyle the leader? [3]

156. In Chester's flashback, what does his dummy tell him to do? [4]

157. Which is the only wonder that Madison didn't master? [3]

158. In which school class is Misty during the 'memory loop' to which she succumbs? [3]

159. What does Scarlett discover that makes her scream until her father comforts her? [5]

160. Why doesn't Mr Wu accept Vendela's initial offer of a threesome? [5]

*See page 86 for the answers*

# EPISODE NAMES – PART 2

*Another ten episodes, another chance to prove you know to which season they belong...*

161. *Chutes and Ladders*

162. *The Ten Commandments Killer*

163. *Unholy Night*

164. *The Replacements*

165. *The Seven Wonders*

166. *Fearful Pranks Ensue*

167. *Battle Royale*

168. *Madness Ends*

169. *The Origins of Monstrosity*

170. *Dark Cousin*

*See page 87 for the answers*

# JUST WHO – PART 2

*More questions that all start with the same word: who...*

171. Who does Charlotte Brown believe herself to be? [2]

172. Who warns the twins that they're going to die in the Murder House? [1]

173. Who does Sally torment alongside the addiction demon? [5]

174. Who does Hank fail to kill in her shack? [3]

175. Who filmed the footage found in the basement by Shelby and Lee? [6]

176. Who proposes the alliance between the voodoo tribe and the witch coven? [3]

177. Who disappears from the back seat of Luke's car, leaving him rather confused? [1]

178. Who does Fiona 'save' from the detectives? [3]

179. Who tells Jon she was with the killer every time he committed a crime? [5]

180. Who is Dandy's favourite cartoon character? [4]

*See page 88 for the answers*

# NAMES – PART 1

*These questions focus on names; for clarity, the questions are asking about names within the show (rather than the name of the actor or actress)...*

181. What was Natacha Rambova's name before she changed it to appear more glamorous? [5]

182. What was the name of the Janes' first victim? [6]

183. What name would Delphine's husband have given to the son he had with Sally? [3]

184. What is Dr Arden's first name (that he uses with 'Arden' rather than his real one)? [2]

185. Name the three surnames that Elizabeth has had of which we are aware. [5]

186. What is Hank Foxx's real name? [3]

187. What is the name of the Nazi that Dr Arden is accused of being? [2]

188. What is Sister Jude's actual birth name? [2]

189. What is the full name of the actress who portrays The Butcher in *My Roanoke Nightmare*? [6]

190. When visiting the American Morbidity Museum, what pseudonym is Maggie going under? [4]

*See page 89 for the answers*

# IT'S ALL ABOUT THE PEOPLE – PART 2

*More character-focused questions here; you should be getting the hang of this now...*

191. From whom is Queenie descended who had a hand in the Salem witch trials? [3]

192. With whom did Elizabeth have a long-lasting lesbian relationship with in the 1970s? [5]

193. On whom did Queenie, alongside Nan and Madison, play a scary prank? [3]

194. When Marcy is forced to sell the house again, who says to her "Good luck selling that lemon"? [1]

195. Is it Kit or Alma who insists they wait until the world is more used to multi-racial couples to reveal their love for one another? [2]

196. Money and Audrey are forced to eat whose flesh? [6]

197. What other name is Elizabeth Short known as? [1]

198. Name the Nazi-hunter (and Holocaust survivor) whom Sister Jude meets with. [2]

199. Whose body does Charles make more 'portable' by cutting it in half at the waist? [1]

200. Name the twin red-headed boys who are murdered by the Infantata. [1]

*See page 90 for the answers*

# OBJECTS – PART 2

*Here's another round of questions focusing on various objects within the show; there's a bit of an illegal drugs theme running through some of these...*

201. In the salon, what does Fiona set on fire? [3]

202. In whose trailer is the missing cop's badge found? [4]

203. What illegal drug does Papa Legba regularly use? [3]

204. The blood of which animal did Fiona use to make it look like the Axeman had killed her? [3]

205. What method of meeting people does Tristan use to invite a man to the hotel? [5]

206. After Twisty's wind-up robot doesn't seem to entertain his captives, what is the next thing he reveals from his bag of tricks? [4]

207. To what drug does Charles Montgomery become addicted? [1]

208. What time does the alarm clock in Vendela's room show when it starts playing jazz music? [5]

209. Who receives the package containing the Minotaur's head? [3]

210. To what drug is Jether rather badly addicted? [6]

*See page 91 for the answers*

# JOBS & OCCUPATIONS

*This round is all about people's jobs; let's see how much you remember...*

211. What public-serving job did Lee have? [6]

212. Prior to becoming the 'twin' on Dandy's own grotesque puppet, what was that person's occupation? [4]

213. With what type of company did Regina hope to work after graduation? [4]

214. After the lies stopped his career as a clown, what did Twisty do to earn a living? [4]

215. What occupation does Lana's partner have? [2]

216. What was Hugo's job? [1]

217. When Shelley cheats on her philandering husband, what is the occupation of the two men whose company she enjoys? [2]

218. What was Dell's particular job in the troupe? [4]

219. Patrick was cheating on Chad; what occupation did the former's new partner have? [1]

220. What was Sister Jude's occupation prior to her calling as a nun? [2]

*See page 92 for the answers*

# NUMBERS — PART 1

*Numerical answers are the focus for this round. Let's see if you have a head for numbers...*

221. At what age did Lee have her first daughter? [6]

222. In which year did Fiona murder the previous Supreme? [3]

223. How many students did Tate kill in his mass shooting? [1]

224. How many Supremes in history have given birth to the next generation's Supreme? [3]

225. Exactly how many of her slaves did Delphine kill? [3]

226. How many people has Jether killed in his life? [6]

227. In which hotel room does Bartholomew reside? [5]

228. How much does Larry try and get out of Ben for headshots in exchange for 'services'? [1]

229. Roughly how much of Larry's body is covered in burns: 20%, 50% or 75%? [1]

230. How many siblings does Regina have? [4]

*See page 93 for the answers*

# LOCATIONS – PART 2

*Most of these questions are more about the 'where' than the 'who' or the 'what'. Got that? Here we go...*

231. In which state is the Roanoke House? [6]

232. What is Violet doing when Leah first picks on her? [1]

233. In which city can we find the school for young witches? [3]

234. What is the school's full name? [3]

235. And when was it built? [3]

236. In what year was the Asylum shut down? [2]

237. In which town does Mike live? [4]

238. Where is Kyle when he strangles Madison? [3]

239. What is the name of the tour that stops outside the Murder House? [1]

240. Where do the Harmons find the rubber man suit? [1]

*See page 94 for the answers*

# RANDOM SELECTION – PART 3

*No introduction needed, so let's get straight on to the questions...*

241. At which university was Dr Elias Cunningham a professor? [6]

242. What does Billie Dean Howard say will happen if a child is conceived by a human woman and ghostly father? [1]

243. What causes Sister Jude to cane Kit? [2]

244. How did Constance become acquainted with Billie Dean Howard? [1]

245. What 'curse' does Zoe suffer from? [3]

246. What is the phrase that Kyle manages to say, learned from his computer game? [3]

247. How does the Axeman discover Fiona's plan to leave without him? [3]

248. The message *I Love You* is seen on a chalk board; from and to whom is it written? [1]

249. When Adelaide asks her mother why she's not like the girls in the magazines, what particular talent is she told that she has? [1]

250. Which human organ is used to make Delphine's 'beauty balm' [3]

*See page 95 for the answers*

# ACTORS AND ACTRESSES – PART 2

*Just like part one of Actors and Actresses, who plays the part of the following characters...*

251. Constance Langdon [1]

252. Bette/Dot Tattler [4]

253. Liz Taylor [5]

254. Delphine LaLaurie [3]

255. Tate Langdon [1]

256. Ethel Darling [4]

257. Will Drake [5]

258. Zoe Benson [3]

259. Sister Jude, [2]

260. Dell Toledo [4]

*See page 96 for the answers*

# QUOTES — PART 2

*More lines that any real fan will recognise instantly – but are you one of them? Time to find out...*

261. "The living cling to life above all, but the trophy misprized is to die in peace." [6]

262. "My brother married one jumpy bitch!" [6]

263. "I was a junkie because I wanted to escape from my mother. You made it so I never can." [5]

264. "My talent has been known to render men speechless, but you'll have to get over it if we are going to work together." [4]

265. "Might I suggest that when you murder him, you would do so *off* the property? It'd be damned awkward to keep running into him for all eternity." [5]

266. "They want to call us monsters? Fine, we'll act like monsters!" [4]

267. "I was a salesman in another life. In this one I am the mother of style. Cut me and I bleed Dior." [5]

268. "Despite appearances, I am not crazy! I am an academic. I am an author." [6]

269. "Did we just marry the devil? 'Cause I don't know if I'm down with' that." [3]

270. "We tell 'em the truth. We visited the twelve most haunted places in America and screwed our brains out in every single one." [2]

*See page 97 for the answers*

# POT LUCK – PART 3

*More questions plucked from the æther that'll require a right old brain-racking. Ready? Let's go...*

271. In the unlikely even Queenie were to go to hell, what would she have to endure? [3]

272. What superstition do the carnies hold about conducting a performance on Halloween? [4]

273. Although Madison does not have a 'unique' power, what skill is she particular good at? [3]

274. What causes churchgoers to accuse Misty of having the power of the devil? [3]

275. Why does Elsa shoot Dell? [4]

276. Name any of the films in which Ramona starred. [5]

277. What does Paul do to relieve his pain after being hit with a knife? [4]

278. What sadistic punishment does Joan give to Luke before locking him in a closet? [3]

279. Why is Spalding mute? [3]

280. Why was Larry supposedly released from prison? [1]

*See page 98 for the answers*

# CHARACTERS – PART 2

*Once again, try to figure out in which season we were first introduced to the following characters...*

281. Dora Brown

282. Bonnie Lipton

283. Scarlett Lowe

284. The Axeman

285. Elizabeth Short

286. Rudolph Valentino

287. The Addiction Demon

288. Queenie

289. Lachlan Drake

290. Luke Ramsey

*See page 99 for the answers*

# WHO AM I? – PART 2

*Try to figure out which character we're talking about here...*

291. After becoming aware of Dr. Arden's experiments, I'm worried that I also could be held accountable. [2]

292. I'm just a simple car salesman who lived in a certain house with his wife and three children. [1]

293. In my youth I used to skin animals, one of the behaviours that led to me spending my formative years in and out of foster homes. [2]

294. When not attending to my duties, I rather enjoy quiet tea parties with my little friends. [3]

295. Back in the day, I could be found hosting elegant parties but my quest for youthful beauty led me to my grave... albeit one in which I would never truly settle. [3]

296. I have more in common with the performers in my wonderful show that you may at first think. [4]

297. When I told my wife I was leaving, she locked herself in our daughters' room and set fire to it. [1]

298. When my wife went away on business trips, I would take the opportunity to slip into the clothing I felt most comfortable in... hers! [5]

299. I'm a very bad Santa. [2]

300. My gift first manifested itself when I was just nine when I found the keys for my nana. [6]

*See page 100 for the answers*

# FOOD & DRINK

*How much attention do you pay to the food and drink featured in the show? There's only one way to find out...*

301. What does the Voodoo Queen's 'love potion' taste like: bitter, sour, sweet or salty? [3]

302. Rather than the orange juice that Alex fetches for him, what does Holden decide to drink? [5]

303. What does Mike insist Jessie call him when he steals her candy? [4]

304. What does Jessie give to Jimmy as a thank-you gift? [4]

305. With what treat does Luke repay Nan for her cake? [3]

306. What medication does Constance add to the cupcakes? [1]

307. After her death, what is Fiona offered for breakfast? [3]

308. What is the recipe with which Iris intends to cleanse Agnetha and Vendela? [5]

309. Whose soup does Myrtle particularly admire? [3]

310. When Queenie visits the Voodoo Queen, what is she cooking? [3]

*See page 101 for the answers*

# EPISODE NAMES – PART 3

*Here's another ten episodes; your job is to decide in which season they were broadcast...*

311. *Blood Bath*

312. *Spilt Milk*

313. *Protect the Coven*

314. *Mommy*

315. *The Sacred Taking*

316. *Pink Cupcakes*

317. *Massacres and Matinees*

318. *Orphans*

319. *Room Service*

320. *The Axeman Cometh*

*See page 102 for the answers*

# JUST WHO – PART 3

*Who, who and more who...*

321. Who does Jessie spot watching her from a bush whilst trick or treating? [4]

322. Who infected Rudolph Valentino? [5]

323. Who looks after the Harmon family dog after they no longer can? [1]

324. Who is sewn into a mattress after receiving a final kiss goodbye? [5]

325. Who does Tristan remind Elizabeth of? [5]

326. Who does Fiona frame for the attack on Cordelia? [3]

327. Who seems strangely relieved when finding out her son 'only' has Measles? [5]

328. Who is Billie Dean Howard trying to contact in the first Séance of hers we see? [1]

329. Who saves Elizabeth after she is shot? [5]

330. Who does Nora tell she will not permit another 'failure' in her house? [1]

*See page 103 for the answers*

# IT'S ALL ABOUT THE PEOPLE – PART 3

*Let's focus purely on the characters of American Horror Story once again...*

331. Which of the witches does Fiona accuse of being the weakest? [3]

332. To whom does Gloria pay an annual homage? [4]

333. From whom is Scathach descended, according to *My Roanoke Nightmare*? [6]

334. With whom does Hank have a one-night-stand after telling his wife he is going to a construction job? [3]

335. Which four characters does Misty resurrect? [3]

336. Which witch notably does not cheer at the announcement of Fiona's appointment as Supreme? [3]

337. Under whose reign as Supreme was Anna Leigh Leighton proclaimed heiress? [3]

338. Which two characters try to warn Will of Elizabeth's intentions at their wedding? [5]

339. Which character is the 'mastermind' behind *My Roanoke Nightmare*? [6]

340. With whom is Mike trapped in the cage? [4]

*See page 104 for the answers*

# RANDOM SELECTION – PART 4

*Round and round it goes, and where it stops nobody knows...*

341. With whom is Dell in love? [4]

342. What event caused Matt and Shelby to move away from Los Angeles? [6]

343. What is Twisty doing whilst Dandy is attempting to saw Maggie in half? [4]

344. What is Desiree's most obvious deformity? [4]

345. Why would Elsa's past lead to her show being cancelled? [4]

346. Name all seven wonders. [3]

347. Patrick helps treat a wound Ben suffers from: how did he get it? [1]

348. How does Madison react to being kicked out of Joan and Luke's house? [3]

349. Under what premise does Violet bring Leah to the Murder House? [1]

350. What was the name of Ambrose's father, the governor of Roanoke? [6]

*See page 105 for the answers*

# OBJECTS – PART 3

*Round three on objects. Some of these are quite easy whereas others will have required a keen eye to spot...*

351. Which of Elizabeth's possessions is Lachlan particularly keen to see? [5]

352. What is to be taken from Monet for the blessed necklace? [6]

353. With what make of gun does Dr Arden end Spivey's life? [2]

354. What does Dr Arden believe the current whereabouts of the Micro-bot to be? [2]

355. What possession of Madison's does Zoe bring to the greenhouse? [3]

356. What accessory does Elizabeth use for killing? [5]

357. Who are the authors of the books that Liz Taylor gives to Tristan? [5]

358. What is the reading on the thermometer after taking Holden's temperature? [5]

359. What classical string instrument does Vivienne play? [1]

360. What is the Hotel's laundress usually seen washing off the sheets? [5]

*See page 106 for the answers*

# LOCATIONS – PART 3

*We've had plenty of 'who', now is the time for a bit of 'where'...*

361. In what town can we find *Fraulein Elsa's Cabinet of Curiosities*? [4]

362. What is the 'theme' of the honeymoon tour on which Leo and his wife are going? [2]

363. What decoration does Larry suggest the parlour would look good with? [1]

364. What is the address of the Murder House? [1]

365. Where was Violet's body hidden by Tate? [1]

366. What is the actual name of the Asylum? [2]

367. Who reclaimed the witches' academy as a school after it had been used as a military hospital in the civil war? [3]

368. What were Chad and Patrick's original intentions for the house? [1]

369. Where and how does Dr Arden Choose to end his life? [2]

370. What is the number of the room to which John takes Elizabeth's head? [5]

*See page 107 for the answers*

# POT LUCK – PART 4

*Another round of questions plucked from the twisted melting pot of American Horror Story general knowledge...*

371. What 'secret' is held by Kyle and his mother? [3]

372. Why did Constance's Hollywood acting career fall by the wayside? [1]

373. Why did Kaylee's ex-fiancée leave her? [3]

374. How does Priscilla make The Butcher let go of Flora? [6]

375. What reason does Monet give for her alcoholism? [6]

376. From which country does Elsa originate? [4]

377. What is particularly unusual about Vivien's twins? [1]

378. Why is smoking a particularly sensitive subject for Leah? [1]

379. Why does Papa Legba refuse a deal with Fiona? [3]

380. How does Kyle discover his body is made from parts that are not his own? [3]

*See page 108 for the answers*

# TRUE OR FALSE

*The concept should be pretty obvious here; a statement is made, but is it true or is it false? You can only choose one...*

381. True or false: although he was a petty thief, Tristan has never been in jail? [5]

382. True or False: Lana accepts the kiss of death? [2]

383. True or false: all of Tristan's targets and victims have been men? [5]

384. True or False: Luke can't have children? [1]

385. True or false: as a child, Johnny Morgan skinned animals, a habit that is said to be present in the formative years of a number of serial killers? [2]

386. True or False: the name of the 'business partner' Hank tells Cordelia has just arrived is Pete Underwood? [3]

387. True or False: Travis draws the line at underwear – no full nudity? [1]

388. True or false: Mama Polk's children are all named after biblical figures? [6]

389. True or false: Scarlett's parents instantly believe her when she tells them that Holden is still alive? [5]

390. True or False: Mary Eunice did not want to die when she was killed by Timothy? [2]

*See page 109 for the answers*

# ΛCTORS ΛND ΛCTRESSES – PΛRT 3

*When the credits roll, are you making a coffee or are you paying attention? If you say the latter, then you can prove it by stating which actor or actress played the part of the following characters...*

391. Spalding [3]

392. Dr. Ben Harmon [1]

393. Iris [5]

394. Violet Harmon [1]

395. John Lowe [5]

396. Kit Walker [2]

397. Desiree Dupree [4]

398. Dr. Oliver Thredson [2]

399. Gloria Mott [4]

400. Alex Lowe [5]

*See page 110 for the answers*

# CHARACTERS – PART 3

*Do old seasons all blur together in your mind? Or is every episode memorised with absolute clarity? We can find out when you decide in which season we're first introduced to each of the following characters...*

401. Pepper

402. Alma Walker

403. Nora Montgomery

404. Regina Ross

405. Papa Legba

406. Twisty

407. Jack Colquitt

408. Marjorie

409. Marie Laveau

410. Edward Mordrake

*See page 111 for the answers*

# RANDOM SELECTION – PART 5

*What? Another random selection so soon? Uh-huh, so answer then these questions ten...*

411. Whilst Fiona becomes Supreme, what position is awarded to Myrtle? [3]

412. Which lie has Dandy been told so that he attends an appointment with Doctor Feinbloom? [4]

413. After being drugged by the twins, where is Dandy when he wakes up? [4]

414. What colour are Madison's eyes? [3]

415. How was the Piggy Man first 'created'? [6]

416. On what date did Lee's first daughter disappear? [6]

417. What is Jessie scared of that Mike exploits on Halloween? [4]

418. What happens to Misty to end her participation in the trial of the seven wonders? [3]

419. Of what does Scarlett tell the therapist that Holden now smells of? [5]

420. How does Jimmy end up paying for a lawyer? [4]

*See page 112 for the answers*

# EPISODE NAMES — PART 4

*You should have this all figured out now; all we need to know is the season in which episodes with the following names were broadcast...*

421. *Afterbirth*

422. *Tricks and Treats*

423. *Go to Hell*

424. *The Coat Hanger*

425. *Show Stoppers*

426. *The Magical Delights of Stevie Nicks*

427. *Room 33*

428. *Head*

429. *Welcome to Briarcliff*

430. *Magical Thinking*

*See page 113 for the answers*

# OBJECTS – PART 4

*You might find some of these a little tricky now, but keep trying your hardest...*

431. During a *Delphi Trust* mission in Northampton, what type of bullets were used to 'subdue' the witches? [3]

432. On which ship has passage allegedly been booked for Dandy? [4]

433. What instrument was the Axeman most famous for playing? [3]

434. What does the spirit board spell out to assist Zoe in finding Madison? [3]

435. What make of phone is Leo holding when he loses the arm carrying it? [2]

436. What tool does Twisty use to kill Bonnie's boyfriend? [4]

437. What is the poultice made of that is used to treat Kyle's stitches? [3]

438. What home-made weapon does Bonnie manage to construct? [4]

439. Shelley married a jazz musician; what instrument did he play? [2]

440. What film does Sister Mary Eunice plan to show in order to calm the inmates over the impending storm? [2]

*See page 114 for the answers*

# JUST WHO – PART 4

*No explanation needed, so let's get on with the questions...*

441. Who takes the fall for Travis's murder? [1]

442. Who tells Queenie that the other witches will never accept her because of her race? [3]

443. Who drowns Nan in the bathtub along with Marie? [3]

444. Who is older: Holden or Scarlet? [5]

445. Who did Chester Creb's wife have an affair with? [4]

446. Who does Chester ask to help him as assistants in his magic act? [4]

447. Who catches Grace and Kit in the kitchen 'in flagrante'? [2]

448. Who gives Charles Montgomery the nickname 'Caspar'? [1]

449. Who helps Charles deliver Vivien's twins? [1]

450. Who materialises in the car seat next to Diana after she quits? [6]

*See page 115 for the answers*

# POT LUCK – PART 5

*Here's a real mix of questions; some easy, some hard, and some fiendishly difficult...*

451. What is Pepper's relationship to Larry? [2]

452. How does Lee escape from Jether? [6]

453. What broken promise particularly angers Priscilla? [6]

454. Which TV Channel is Billie Dean Howard supposedly filming a Reality TV show for? [1]

455. What unusual one-off show did Ethel partake in to raise money? [4]

456. Why was Pepper put into the Asylum? [2]

457. Why did Mason divorce Lee? [6]

458. What procedure does Charles Montgomery offer that causes plenty of women to come to his house? [1]

459. When Cricket has trouble concentrating whilst at Roanoke House, what does he do to get his wits together? [6]

460. How is the new book being written by Dr Cunningham described? [6]

*See page 116 for the answers*

# NAMES – PART 2

*Here's your second names round. Once again, we should point out that the questions are asking about names within the show (rather than the name of the actor or actress)...*

461. What is Chester's Ventriloquist's Dummy called? [4]

462. What is Fiona's full name? [3]

463. What is the Voodoo Queen's 'real' name? [3]

464. What was the name of Lee's first daughter? [6]

465. What is the name of Edward Mott's slave/lover? [6]

466. What was the Minotaur's 'real' name? [3]

467. What is Delphine's oldest daughter known as? [3]

468. Name Corey's parents. [4]

469. What is Ethel's ex-husband called? [4]

470. What is Marie's full name? [3]

*See page 117 for the answers*

# QUOTES – PART 3

*So are the following quotes lines of dialogue that stuck in your mind, or are you staring at the page blankly thinking "I don't remember that at all"? Let's see...*

471. "Childish? Hell, I'm the Queen of Candyland!" [2]

472. "There is only one law here; the bigger the star, the bigger the tent." [4]

473. "If you're trying to kill yourself cut vertically. They can't stitch that up." [1]

474. "I grew up on white girl shit like Charmed and Sabrina the Teenage Witch." [3]

475. "I'm not naïve to the ways of men. Their need to objectify, conquer. They see what they want to see. Women however see into the soul of a person." [1]

476. "Surprise, bitch! I bet you thought you'd seen the last of me!" [3]

477. "I have long stopped asking why the mad do mad things." [1]

478. "You're a cheater! Young girls, old ladies with feather dusters. You're so weird and pathetic I'm surprised you haven't gone after me." [1]

479. "Tell me, young man, have you ever heard of the term 'gay for pay'?" [6]

480. "Do you think it's possible to take someone's power by eating their flesh?" [4]

*See page 118 for the answers*

# WHO AM I? – PART 3

*One more chance to guess which character is being described in each paragraph below. Think carefully now...*

481. One of the residents at the Hotel Cortez, you could say I have two mommys... [5]

482. Banished! Banished by my own blood and left in the forest to starve. But revenge was mine and now all of our souls belong to the land... forever! [6]

483. During the trial of the Seven Wonders I end up stuck, unable to bring myself back from a hellish childhood memory. [3]

484. I'm a fundamentalist Christian who takes absolutely no pleasure in punishing my son. Nope, none at all. [3]

485. I'm the mastermind behind a smash hit show, but the sequel will be even better. *I* say the camera never stops, no matter what! [6]

486. Handsome yet emotionally and psychologically disturbed, you could say money and madness are a family trait of mine. [4]

487. We're forced to live our lives closer than most people would ever understand, but our personalities couldn't be further apart. [4]

488. I was the sole survivor of a massacre and even so I ended up losing my daughter. [6]

489. There's a hotel that is the location of some rather unusual goings on; you'll find me there at the front desk. [5]

490. After years of being called an ugly monster I lived out my last remaining hours as a 'pretty girl' wearing a mask that mother got for me. Halloween... what a day to die! [1]

*See page 119 for the answers*

# WHOSE DEATH IS THIS? – PART 2

*Time once again to decide which characters ceased to be, finding themselves bereft of life having shuffled off their mortal coils in the ways described below...*

491. Admiring the view in a delirious state, then pushed from the window, falling several floors to an unpleasant fate. [5]

492. Ironically killed by a former lover after contemplating suicide. [1]

493. The first freak to die during Dandy's psychotic murderous rampage. [4]

494. Although only one is tossed over the landing of the staircase, two happen to meet their death. [2]

495. The tenth commandment... or is it actually the sixth? [5]

496. Gunned down in their bedroom by a SWAT team after a spree which took the lives of many students. [1]

497. The victim of a classic magic trick with a twist – and from which there is no escape. [4]

498. Smothered with a pillow at mother's request... not that she would ever admit it. [1]

499. Overdosed on sleeping pills after being overwhelmed with emotion. [1]

500. Curtains close on this freak's life from the expert throw of just one knife – and after all those years of friendship! [4]

*See page 120 for the answers*

# RANDOM SELECTION – PART 6

*A great selection here; let's see how well you do...*

501. Why does Charles Montgomery give Elizabeth a 'Chelsea Smile'? [1]

502. With what words did Mordrake's second face spare Ethel? [4]

503. How is Kyle immune to Zoe's Black Widow power? [3]

504. What does Shelley do to make Doctor Arden amputate her legs? [2]

505. What happened to Leigh in his cell when the guards were carolling? [2]

506. What event caused Mary Eunice to be traumatized as a teenager? [2]

507. What lie was spread about Twisty that prevented him working as a clown? [4]

508. What does Fiona bring the Voodoo Queen when offering an allegiance? [3]

509. Sally's heroin doesn't kill Iris – so how does Sally then 'help out'? [5]

510. Of what three things is Papa Legba the god? [3]

*See page 121 for the answers*

# COSTUMES

*A special round now focusing on clothing and costumes. Here's ten questions for the fashion-conscious fan...*

511. What, belonging to Wendy, is added to the Bloody Face costume? [2]

512. One night in December, Leigh killed eighteen people from five different families as well as a charity collector dressed as what? [2]

513. When Tate is in the rocking chair waiting for Leah, what does the slogan on his shirt read? [1]

514. In what clothes did Sally die? [5]

515. What is Max Ellison wearing after having feasted on his parents? [5]

516. What's the name of the security firm on Luke's badge? [1]

517. When Tristan accompanies Elizabeth to a Halloween party, who does he dress up as? [5]

518. Which witch is particularly fond of fashionable gloves and vintage cat-eye glasses? [3]

519. What unusual transformation happens to Shachath when she 'kindly' gives someone the kiss of death? [2]

520. What are the two main colours in Mike's clown outfit? [4]

*See page 122 for the answers*

# LOCATIONS – PART 4

*And on to your next locations round...*

521. To where is Elizabeth invited to vacation with Will and Lachlan? [5]

522. In which room does Scarlett ask Holden if he remembers their parents? [5]

523. At which lake did Twisty kill Bonnie's boyfriend? [4]

524. Who is the first person to use the name 'The Murder House'? [1]

525. From which country did Grace move to America as a young girl? [2]

526. Where does Fiona tell Spalding to bury Fiona? [3]

527. In what type of vehicle is Twisty's cage? [4]

528. Name the fast food outlet where Queenie used to work. [3]

529. Moira wants Joe to put in a pool (thus unearthing her body), but what does he actually intend to do? [1]

530. For whom did Charles Montgomery build the Murder House? [1]

*See page 123 for the answers*

# NUMBERS – PART 2

*Another special numbers round now; don't worry though, you don't have to be a mathematician to answer these – like most other questions you just need a good memory and an eye (or ear) for detail...*

531. How many days per fortnight did Flora's mother have custody of her? [6]

532. How many metres does the producer request the actress portraying The Butcher to be away from the set? [6]

533. How many minutes is Hank given alone with Cordelia by the hospital nurse? [3]

534. How many Salem descendants had Hank killed in the prior three years undercover work? [3]

535. For how much do Dandy and his mother wish to purchase the twins? [4]

536. Hazel mentions there was a terrible accident in a particular room – which number was it? [5]

537. On what date did Hazel Evers lose her son Albert? [5]

538. Roughly how many patients died within the walls of the Asylum during its time as a tuberculosis ward: 13,000, 46,000 or 128,000? [2]

539. How much does Cricket want for finding Flora? [6]

540. How many children did Constance say she had? [1]

*See page 124 for the answers*

# DEATH & KILLING — PART 2

*More marvellous morose morbidity...*

541. How did Angela and Margaret die? [1]

542. How did Joan kill her wealthy husband? [3]

543. How is Joan herself killed? [3]

544. How would people supposedly be safe from the Axeman's killing spree? [3]

545. What did the Axeman do with Cordelia's mother's body? [3]

546. How does Cordelia figure out where Misty is buried? [3]

547. How is Elias Cunningham 'finished off'? [6]

548. What does Mama Polk do to avenge her son Cain's death? [6]

549. Why does Lee believe the charred body is Mason? [6]

550. Why is Lee acquitted of murder? [6]

*See page 125 for the answers*

# OBJECTS – PART 5

*You're surely getting the hang of these now, so on with the quiz...*

551. Hallie wasn't actually put in the microwave – so what did Hayden use to achieve the effect? [1]

552. What belonging of Patrick's is needed for the Pagan ritual? [1]

553. With what weapon does Zoe deal with most of the dead? [3]

554. Who actually purchased the rubber man suit? [1]

555. Name the make and model of Leo's camera [2]

556. What does Monsignor Timothy Howard use to end Shelley's suffering? [2]

557. What drug did Sally sell to Donovan prior to her arrival at the hotel? [5]

558. With what implement does Sister Jude successfully fend off Leigh? [2]

559. What item does Sister Jude use to get Dr Arden's fingerprints? [2]

560. What does Elizabeth give to the detective to help find Rudolph Valentino? [5]

*See page 126 for the answers*

# CHARACTERS – PART 4

*One last time, in which season were the following characters introduced...*

561. Mother Claudia

562. Max Ellison

563. Charlotte Brown

564. Chad Warwick

565. Missy Stone

566. Tristan Duffy

567. Teresa Morrison

568. Lorraine Harvey

569. Hank Foxx

570. Leigh Emerson

*See page 127 for the answers*

# ACTORS AND ACTRESSES — PART 4

*Also the last of these rounds, just name the real-life person who plays these roles...*

571. Misty Day [3]

572. Kyle Spencer [3]

573. Donovan [5]

574. Myrtle Snow [3]

575. Larry Harvey [1]

576. Lana Winters [2]

577. Stanley [4]

578. Monsignor Timothy Howard [2]

579. Cordelia Foxx [3]

580. Fiona Goode [3]

*See page 128 for the answers*

# IT'S ALL ABOUT THE PEOPLE – PART 4

*Back to the focus on the characters in the show; here's ten more questions for you...*

581. With which character does Queenie have a sexual encounter that leaves her greatly the worse for wear? [3]

582. Which three characters escape from the Asylum, but have to turn back after encountering the raspers? [2]

583. To whom was Pepper married in a mock ceremony? [4]

584. From whose body does the demon 'jump' to Sister Mary Eunice's? [2]

585. Name the rapper who was turned by Ramona (his rapper name). [5]

586. Zoe walks in on Madison whilst she is getting amorous with whom? [3]

587. Which officer's disappearance leads to Jack Colquitt brandishing a warrant to search the premises? [4]

588. With whom did the Voodoo Queen strike a deal to exchange her soul for immortality? [3]

589. Into whose luggage does Bartholomew fall? [5]

590. To which two people is Papa Legba speaking when he says "You two, together, big trouble"? [3]

*See page 129 for the answers*

# EPISODE NAMES – PART 5

*The final episode-naming round now; just decide in which season episodes with the following names were broadcast...*

591. *Curtain Call*

592. *Piggy Piggy*

593. *Open House*

594. *The Dead*

595. *Bullseye*

596. *Devil's Night*

597. *Monsters Among Us*

598. *The Name Game*

599. *Test of Strength*

600. *Home Invasion*

*See page 130 for the answers*

# POT LUCK – PART 6

*And now back once again to some pot luck questions...*

601. At what event did Matt Miller meet his future wife? [6]

602. What procedure does Dr Arden suggest for Charlotte? [2]

603. What condition is Ethel told she has by Doctor Bonham? [4]

604. What does Dandy offer Jack Colquitt to overlook his crimes? [4]

605. In what room does Marie suggest her talents lie? [3]

606. What is Todd Connors' connection to *My Roanoke Nightmare*? [6]

607. Who kidnaps Flora and why? [6]

608. Which moon enables ghosts to murder at will? [6]

609. What does Stanley offer to the twins that thankfully they decline? [4]

610. What two key factors lead to Chad's meltdown when he demands Ben and Vivien leave the house? [1]

*See page 131 for the answers*

# JUST WHO – PART 5

*Now the final 'who' round. Keep going, you're nearly at the end of the quiz...*

611. Who was Delphine's final husband? [3]

612. Who initiated the attack on Cordelia that left her blind? [3]

613. Who abducted Holden from the Merry-go-round? [5]

614. Who is shot by the bullets intended for Nan? [3]

615. Who was Elizabeth's accountant? [5]

616. Who destroys Ben's car so he can't take Vivien to the hospital? [1]

617. Who stopped Elizabeth from throwing herself out of a window? [5]

618. Who is described as 'the most exotic woman in the whole world'? [5]

619. Who does Dandy have framed for the murders? [4]

620. Who does Marcy describe as 'perverts'? [1]

*See page 132 for the answers*

# RANDOM SELECTION – PART 7

*And this is it, the very last round. Let's see if you can finish on a high...*

621. What 'type' of witch is Kaylee? [3]

622. Name the two characters from the show who have both said they surrounded themselves with the white spirit light.

623. When Timothy pleads for help from Shachath, with what words does she reply? [2]

624. What does Madison 'suggest' as the reason Spalding is mute? [3]

625. Of what entity is Ben's patient Derek extremely terrified? [1]

626. What fashion label is one of the last words uttered by Myrtle? [3]

627. Which award is the actress playing The Butcher nominated for? [6]

628. What does Twisty reveal to Mordrake is his motivation? [4]

629. What happens to Derek when he repeats his feared mantra into his bathroom mirror? [1]

630. What mistake does Zoe make, ending her participation in the Seven Wonders trial? [3]

*See page 133 for the answers*

# THE ANSWERS

# ABOUT THE SHOW

1. *Murder House, Asylum, Coven, Freak Show, Hotel* and *Roanoke*

2. Ryan Murphy and Brad Falchuk

3. 21st December 2011

4. Episode 1 of *Freak show*, which was seen by 6.13 million people

5. 59

6. Jessica Lange

7. 3 – *Coven*, narrowly beating *Freak Show*

8. Lady Gaga

9. *Meet the Residents*

10. Halloween Horror Nights

# POT LUCK – PART 1

11. He blew his bottom jaw off with a shotgun in an attempted suicide

12. Her drinking, sexual promiscuity and (believed) manslaughter

13. L.A. Homes Realty

14. Vitalum Vitalis

15. He pops one of his balloon animals

16. She attempts to shave her head

17. She can no longer hear her thoughts

18. Her singing ability

19. He was dropped on his head as a baby

20. Making him sit on a toilet seat lined with nails

# JUST WHO – PART 1

21. Teresa

22. Zoe

23. Diana Cross

24. Jether

25. Pepper

26. Larry Harvey

27. Sister Mary Eunice

28. Shelby

29. Travis

30. Rory Monahan

31. *The Price is Right*

32. To prevent him from seeing Donovan's naked body

33. He said she wasn't able to follow directions

34. A masked intruder

35. The Devil

36. *A Closer Walk With Thee*

37. MURDE

38. 1904

39. Parade

40. She was tricked into partaking in a snuff film during which they were removed with a chainsaw

# EPISODE NAMES — PART 1

41. *Coven*

42. *Hotel*

43. *Coven*

44. *Murder House*

45. *Hotel*

46. *Murder House*

47. *Asylum*

48. *Murder House*

49. *Coven*

50. *Freak Show*

# IT'S ALL ABOUT THE PEOPLE — PART 1

51. Missy Stone

52. Twisty's

53. Stevie Nicks

54. Kit Walker

55. Elias Cunningham's

56. Dandy

57. Ramona

58. John's

59. Sally Freeman

60. Hallie

# ACTORS AND ACTRESSES – PART 1

61. Emma Roberts

62. Connie Britton

63. James Cromwell

64. Angela Bassett

65. Lily Rabe

66. Lizzie Brocheré

67. Jessica Lange

68. Evan Peters

69. Lady Gaga

70. Emma Roberts

# OBJECTS — PART 1

71. A genuine Sasquatch foetus

72. The Book of Revelations

73. It is not big enough for the sins she has committed

74. Agnetha

75. TAInT

76. He preferred leather to latex

77. A candlestick

78. Oxygen-infused laundry soap

79. She has a full set to sell on eBay, and Moira is fired

80. Dot's diary

# CHARACTERS – PART 1

81. *Coven*

82. *Murder House*

83. *Asylum*

84. *Freak Show*

85. *Hotel*

86. *Murder House*

87. *Asylum*

88. *Hotel*

89. *Murder House / Hotel*

90. *Coven*

# WHO AM I? – PART 1

91. Lana Winters

92. Bartholomew

93. Sister Jude

94. Nora Montgomery

95. Cordelia Foxx / Goode

96. Scathach

97. Priscilla

98. Maggie Esmerelda

99. Edward Mordrake

100. Tristan Duffy

# LOCATIONS – PART 1

101. Mott Manor

102. A hair salon

103. Bad juju

104. A fast-food restaurant

105. Their doorbells, which play the same chime

106. Fast & Furious

107. The Thatcher Boarding School

108. To visit Universal Studios

109. Puerto Rico

110. Cordelia's car

# QUOTES – PART 1

111. Lana Winters

112. Sister Mary Eunice

113. Oliver Thredson

114. Ambrose White

115. Vivien Harmon

116. Sally McKenna

117. Fiona Goode

118. Elizabeth / Countess

119. Maggie Esmerelda

120. Delphine LaLaurie

# WHOSE DEATH IS THIS? – PART 1

121. Dandy Mott

122. Maddison Montgomery

123. Johnny Morgan

124. Natacha Rambova

125. Shelley

126. Kyle Spencer

127. Will Drake

128. Zoe Benson

129. Myrtle Snow

130. Arthur Arden

# RANDOM SELECTION – PART 2

131. A couple of days

132. *Spirit Chasers*

133. Reading her erotica novels in peace

134. To open Luke's front door

135. Missing children

136. Holds a lighter flame to her hand and eats the entire contents of the fridge

137. Her soul

138. A fatal accident at a frat party

139. Throwing knives at a dummy being rotated on a wheel

140. To store Edward Mott's art collection

141. Shot in the head (for refusing to take her poisoned medicine)

142. Sawing them in half

143. At least a week

144. She hides in her trailer

145. Measles

146. By pushing her through a window so she fell to her death

147. She disconnected her respirator

148. She didn't want him taken away by child protection services

149. Chopped it up and fed it to the dogs.

150. He is actually still a living creature who has sustained himself since his 'creation' by eating possums and bugs

# POT LUCK – PART 2

151. *September Song*

152. By Alex's blood injected into his IV

153. Myrtle

154. The wild boar's raw heart

155. Kappa Lambda Gamma

156. Kill his wife

157. Divination

158. Science

159. Two disembowelled men

160. He thinks that she and Agnetha are prostitutes determined to 'tag team' him, charging him for the night

# EPISODE NAMES — PART 2

161. *Hotel*

162. *Hotel*

163. *Asylum*

164. *Coven*

165. *Coven*

166. *Coven*

167. *Hotel*

168. *Asylum*

169. *Asylum*

170. *Asylum*

# JUST WHO – PART 2

171. Anne Frank

172. Addy

173. Gabriel

174. Misty Day

175. Dr Cunningham

176. Fiona

177. Hayden

178. Madison and Zoe

179. Wren

180. Woody the Woodpecker

# NAMES – PART 1

181. Winifred Hudnut

182. Margaret

183. Pierre

184. Arthur

185. Johnson, March and Drake

186. Henry Renard

187. Hans Gruper

188. Judy Martin

189. Agnes Mary Winstead

190. Miss Rothschild

# IT'S ALL ABOUT THE PEOPLE – PART 2

191. Tituba

192. Ramona Royale

193. Zoe Benson

194. Constance

195. Alma

196. Lee's

197. The Black Dahlia

198. Sam Goodman

199. Elizabeth Short's

200. Troy and Bryan

# OBJECTS – PART 2

201. A shelf of wigs

202. Meep's

203. Cocaine

204. A goat

205. Grindr

206. The store clerk's head

207. Ether

208. 2:25 a.m.

209. Chantal

210. Cocaine

# JOBS & OCCUPATIONS

211. A police officer

212. An Avon lady's

213. A law firm

214. Made novelties from junk

215. School teacher

216. A car salesman

217. Sailors in the navy

218. The strongman

219. Trainer at the gym

220. A nightclub singer

# NUMBERS – PART 1

221. Seventeen

222. 1971

223. Fifteen

224. Just one – Fiona

225. 62

226. None

227. 33

228. $1000

229. 0.75

230. None – she is an only child

# LOCATIONS — PART 2

231. North Carolina

232. Smoking in a public area

233. New Orleans, Louisiana

234. Miss Robichaux's Academy for Exceptional Young Ladies

235. 1790

236. 1971

237. West Beach, Florida

238. The greenhouse

239. The Eternal Darkness Horror Tour

240. In the attic

# RANDOM SELECTION – PART 3

241. Bradley University

242. It would be the antichrist and would bring about the end of the world

243. He spits on her

244. Through Craigslist

245. Anyone she has intercourse with suffers from a fatal aneurysm

246. This road goes two ways

247. He finds a plane ticket in her bag

248. From Tate to Violet

249. Finger painting

250. Pancreases

# ACTORS AND ACTRESSES — PART 2

251. Jessica Lange

252. Sarah Paulson

253. Denis O'Hare

254. Kathy Bates

255. Evan Peters

256. Kathy Bates

257. Cheyenne Jackson

258. Taissa Farmiga

259. Jessica Lange

260. Michael Chiklis

# QUOTES – PART 2

261. Edward Philippe Mott

262. Lee Miller/Harris

263. Donovan

264. Elsa Mars

265. James March

266. Jimmy Darling

267. Liz Taylor

268. Elias Cunningham

269. Zoe Benson

270. Leo Morrison

271. Serving customers in a fast food restaurant forever

272. That even the most trivial one will summon Mordrake, who must take one of them back to the grave with him

273. Telekinesis

274. She resurrects a bird from the dead

275. He confesses what he did to Ma Petite

276. *Slaughter Sister, Silky Fine,* or *Bride of Blackenstein*

277. Smokes opium

278. She gives him a bleach enema

279. He removed his own tongue

280. He had terminal brain cancer

# CHARACTERS – PART 2

281. *Freak Show*

282. *Freak Show*

283. *Hotel*

284. *Coven*

285. *Murder House*

286. *Hotel*

287. *Hotel*

288. *Coven / Hotel*

289. *Hotel*

290. *Coven*

# WHO AM I? – PART 2

291. Timothy Howard

292. Hugo Langdon

293. Johnny Morgan

294. Spalding

295. Delphine LaLaurie

296. Elsa Mars

297. Larry Harvey

298. Liz Taylor

299. Leigh Emerson

300. Cricket Marlowe

# FOOD & DRINK

301. Sweet

302. The family dog's blood

303. Master Mike

304. A plate of home-made brownies

305. Cookies

306. Ipecac syrup

307. Catfish

308. Blended organ meats and white wine

309. Delphine's

310. Gumbo

# EPISODE NAMES – PART 3

311. *Freak Show*

312. *Asylum*

313. *Coven*

314. *Hotel*

315. *Coven*

316. *Freak Show*

317. *Freak Show*

318. *Freak Show*

319. *Hotel*

320. *Coven*

# JUST WHO — PART 3

321. Twisty

322. Friedrich Wilhelm Murnau

323. Marcy

324. Gabriel

325. Rudolph Valentino

326. Myrtle

327. Mrs. Ellison

328. Addy

329. Sally

330. Ben

# IT'S ALL ABOUT THE PEOPLE – PART 3

331. Zoe

332. Doris Duke

333. The Druids and their Roman conquerors

334. Kaylee

335. Myrtle, Madison, Joan and herself

336. Myrtle

337. Mimi DeLongpre

338. Mrs Evers and Mr March

339. Sidney Aaron James

340. Bonnie and Corey

# RANDOM SELECTION — PART 4

341. A prostitute by the name of Andy

342. They were attacked when out walking one evening, which caused Shelby to miscarry

343. Playing a toy piano

344. She has three breasts

345. She had a 'morals clause' in her contract

346. Divination, Telekinesis, Pyrokinesis, Concilium, Transmutation, Descensum and Vitalis Vitalum

347. Cutting pumpkins

348. She sets the curtains on fire

349. To sell her cocaine

350. John White

# OBJECTS – PART 3

351. Her vinyl records

352. A tooth

353. A Luger P08

354. Inside Kit's body

355. Her gun

356. Her chain mail glove

357. Bronte and Wilde

358. 75 degrees

359. The 'cello

360. Blood

# LOCATIONS – PART 3

361. Jupiter, Florida

362. Visiting various landmarks of murder

363. Murals

364. 939 Berro Drive, LA 90068

365. In the crawl space

366. Briarcliffe Manor

367. Marion Warton

368. To redecorate and sell on at a profit.

369. In a cremation oven with the woman he loved

370. 64

371. She has been abusing him

372. She objected to the nudity that was 'flooding the industry'

373. Because she was 'weird'

374. She hits her in the head

375. The audience's dislike for her character, which turned into dislike for her

376. Germany

377. They both have different fathers

378. Her grandmother died of lung cancer

379. She has no soul

380. He sees tattoos that he knows belonged to his friends

# TRUE OR FALSE

381. False – he has

382. False – she changes her mind at the last minute

383. True

384. True – he reveals this to Ben.

385. True

386. False – it is Phil Underwood

387. False – he's willing to do anything to become famous

388. True

389. False – they don't believe her at al.

390. False: She was tired of living with the Demon

# ACTORS AND ACTRESSES – PART 3

391. Denis O'Hare

392. Dylan McDermott

393. Kathy Bates

394. Taissa Farmiga

395. Wes Bentley

396. Evan Peters

397. Angela Bassett

398. Zachary Quinto

399. Frances Conroy

400. Chloë Sevigny

# CHARACTERS — PART 3

401. *Asylum (but is also in Freak Show)*

402. *Asylum*

403. *Murder House*

404. *Freak Show*

405. *Coven*

406. *Freak Show*

407. *Murder House (but is also in Freak Show)*

408. *Freak Show*

409. *Coven*

410. *Freak Show*

# RANDOM SELECTION – PART 5

411. Head of the Witches Council

412. That his genius level IQ is to be tested

413. In Houdini's water tank

414. Hazel

415. He was a deserter forced to wear a pigs head and tail (then roasted like a hog) after stealing from the colony's storehouse

416. 4th of July

417. Clowns

418. She can't come back from the afterlife

419. Lavender

420. By selling his hands

# EPISODE NAMES – PART 4

421. *Murder House*

422. *Asylum*

423. *Coven*

424. *Asylum*

425. *Freak Show*

426. *Coven*

427. *Hotel*

428. *Coven*

429. *Asylum*

430. *Freak Show*

# OBJECTS — PART 4

431. Blessed bullets

432. The Queen Mary

433. Saxophone

434. Attic

435. An iPhone

436. A pair of shears

437. Moss and alligator dung

438. A plank with a nail in it

439. Bass

440. *The Sign of the Cross*

# JUST WHO – PART 4

441. Larry

442. Delphine

443. Fiona

444. Holden

445. Their next door neighbour, Alice

446. Dot and Bette

447. Sister Mary Eunice

448. Hayden

449. Maria and Gladys

450. The Piggy Man

# POT LUCK – PART 5

451. He is her brother-in-law

452. By 'seducing' him to the point he can choke then stab him

453. That The Butcher intends to kill Flora first instead of last

454. Lifetime

455. People could watch her giving birth

456. She was framed for murder by Rita and Larry

457. Because of her alcohol and painkiller addiction

458. Abortions

459. He goes for a walk in the woods

460. A true crime novel in the vein of Helter Skelter

# NAMES – PART 2

461. Marjorie

462. Fiona Borgia Vandenheuvel Goode

463. Marie Laveau

464. Emily

465. Guinness

466. Bastien

467. Borquita

468. Jeffrey and Mildred

469. Dell

470. Marie Louise Pauline LaLaurie

# QUOTES – PART 3

471. Sister Jude

472. Bette Tattler

473. Tate Langdon

474. Queenie

475. Moira O'Hara

476. Madison Montgomery

477. Constance Langdon

478. Violet Harmon

479. Cricket Marlowe

480. Dandy Mott

# WHO AM I? — PART 3

481. Holden Lowe

482. The Butcher / Thomasin White

483. Misty Day

484. Joan Ramsey

485. Sidney Aaron James

486. Dandy Mott

487. Bette and Dot Tattler

488. Lee Miller/Harris

489. Iris

490. Adelaide Langdon

# WHOSE DEATH IS THIS? – PART 2

491. Sally McKenna

492. Ben Harmon

493. Paul

494. Sister Mary Eunice

495. Elizabeth / Countess

496. Tate Langdon

497. Maggie Esmerelda

498. Beauregard Langdon

499. Violet Harmon

500. Ethel Darling

501. She 'looked so sad'.

502. "Not the one"

503. He has already died once

504. She laughs at his penis

505. He was raped by five other men

506. A typical teenage skinny dipping prank

507. That he was molesting children

508. Delphine's head

509. She kills her with a plastic bag

510. Travel, opportunity and luck

# COSTUMES

511. Her teeth

512. Santa Claus

513. Normal People Scare Me

514. A leopard/cheetah print coat over a purple mini dress

515. A pirate costume

516. Heirloom Security

517. Dracula

518. Myrtle

519. She sprouts wings

520. Purple and green

# LOCATIONS — PART 4

521. Paris

522. The game room

523. Lake Okeechobee

524. Stan (the tour guide)

525. France

526. Deep below the lawn

527. An old abandoned bus

528. Chubby's

529. Pave the land as a parking lot.

530. His wife, Nora

# NUMBERS – PART 2

531. Three

532. 150

533. Fifteen

534. Nine

535. $15,000

536. 51

537. Halloween 1925

538. 46000

539. $25,000

540. Four – although only three are actually 'revealed' in the show

# DEATH & KILLING – PART 2

541. Their mother set their bedroom on fire

542. Putting bees in his car thus triggering an allergic reaction

543. She is 'forced' to drink a bottle of bleach by Nan

544. By playing jazz music

545. He fed it to the alligators

546. She touches an article of her clothing

547. Lot beats him over the head with a hammer

548. She break's Shelby's ankle with a hammer

549. She recognises the jewellery taken from it

550. Her behaviour is believed to be due to a hallucinogenic form of marijuana found on the farm

# OBJECTS — PART 5

551. A tomato

552. His ring

553. A chainsaw

554. Chad

555. Leica M-7

556. His rosary beads

557. Heroin

558. A letter opener

559. A glass (having proposed a celebratory toast)

560. His cards

# CHARACTERS — PART 4

561. *Asylum*

562. *Hotel*

563. *Asylum*

564. *Murder House*

565. *Asylum*

566. *Hotel*

567. *Asylum*

568. *Murder House*

569. *Coven*

570. *Asylum*

# ACTORS AND ACTRESSES – PART 4

571. Lily Rabe

572. Evan Peters

573. Matt Bomer

574. Frances Conroy

575. Denis O'Hare

576. Sarah Paulson

577. Denis O'Hare

578. Joseph Fiennes

579. Sarah Paulson

580. Jessica Lange

# IT'S ALL ABOUT THE PEOPLE – PART 4

581. Bastien

582. Grace, Shelley and Kit

583. Salty

584. Jed Potter's

585. Prophet Moses

586. Kyle

587. Detective Bunch

588. Papa Legba

589. John Lowe's

590. Marie and Fiona

# EPISODE NAMES – PART 5

591. *Freak Show*

592. *Murder House*

593. *Murder House*

594. *Coven*

595. *Freak Show*

596. *Hotel*

597. *Freak Show*

598. *Asylum*

599. *Freak Show*

600. *Murder House*

# POT LUCK – PART 6

601. A yoga class

602. A transorbital lobotomy

603. Cirrhosis of the liver

604. A million dollars

605. The boudoir

606. He created a website and social media account dedicated to the series

607. Priscilla – to keep her safe from The Butcher

608. The blood moon

609. A cupcake laced with poison

610. Their costumes are sub-par and they bought the 'wrong apples' for the bobbing station.

# JUST WHO — PART 5

611. Louis LaLaurie

612. Harrison Renard

613. Elizabeth

614. Joan and Luke

615. Bernie Madoff

616. Troy and Bryan

617. James Patrick March

618. Natacha Rambova

619. Lobster boy

620. Chad and Patrick

621. Pyrokinetic

622. Billie Dean Howard and Misty Day

623. I'm here

624. His tongue was cut off because he was bad at giving oral sex

625. Piggy Man

626. Balenciaga

627. A Saturn award

628. Keeping children 'safe' from their mean chore-giving parents

629. He is shot and killed by an armed robber

630. She impales herself on the gate

*If you liked this quiz, you may also enjoy...*

UNOFFICIAL & UNAUTHORISED

THE
SEASONS 1-6

# WALKING DEAD
## ULTIMATE QUIZ BOOK

JACK GOLDSTEIN & FRANKIE TAYLOR

CPSIA information can be obtained
at www.ICGtesting.com
Printed in the USA
LVHW032057010119
602325LV00001B/15/P

9 781785 386152